A Play Of Words

By Deepika. M

notionpress.com

INDIA • SINGAPORE • MALAYSIA

ISBN 979-8-88869-025-3

Dedication

To Amma, for being the strongest person I know.

To Daddy, for being the best Dad a girl can hope
to have.

To Jhanani, for being the most amazing sister and my
best friend.

To Rana and Mithra, for your amazing smiles and truest
love.

To myself.

And,

To you.

Welcome to my book.

It means to me quite a lot,

That you chose to pick this one,

From the rest of the lot.

Some of these were spontaneous,

Some, less so,

But each of them I treasure and hold dear,

And I'm ecstatic to share them with you.

Contents

———• *Contents* •·—

Point of View

1 An Animal's Vomit

Eating an animal's vomit is weird, but not if it's a bee's,

Bacteria in your food is bad, unless it's curd or cheese.

Punching invisible targets makes you crazy, unless
you're in a gym,

Splashes of paint on the clothes is a grim mess, but
worth millions on a canvas.

They say white is good for weddings, but that's not
true where I'm from,

Maybe things are good only based on where and
when you are.

Bell-bottoms were all-in, but wear it now and
you're insane,

I wonder if some time from now my little black dress
will be called the same.

We humans are a strange lot, I'm not sure if you'd agree,

But to me, wasting paper to print "stop cutting down
trees", and a species that wages wars for peace seems
somewhat slightly strange.

Maybe we are crazy, or maybe it's just me,

Only time will tell which is which, and show what
remains to be seen.

But time is strange, that, I don't care if you agree,

If like me, life has treated you with something unique,
you too will agree.

If it hasn't, wait your turn; you will get there eventually,

If you're in your few last breaths and still don't see,
then maybe it's because not all of us were meant
to agree.

Time is interesting; in the grand scheme of things, human life is so brief that we can't even be called a helpless witness to time. That itself would be too great of an overestimation. Time helps an oak out of an acorn, breaks bonds thought to be unbreakable, carves canyons onto the face of the earth, and heals wounds we thought would never stop hurting, all with equal ease.

Fashion is the easiest example to trace time's trend. Clothing trends and styles change rapidly with time, sometimes cyclically, circling around every couple of years, with what's in and what's not changing frequently. Little black dresses were one of the most modern and 'on trend' outfits back when I wrote this poem. I thought that they were new and 'Oh, so cool'. Little did I know that they were originally 'New' and 'Oh, so cool' way back in the 1920s. Who knows? Maybe bell-bottoms are in again?

2 A Confession

To those who buy this book,

I have a confession to make,

I make no promises to tell epic tales.

I know no truths that haven't already been said,

So, if it's a secret you are searching for,

This isn't your best bet.

I write because I want to,

I was never trained in the arts,

I write what comes from my brain,

And sometimes, my heart.

I want to know, but don't yet know, what an iambic pentameter is,

And sometimes, I'm not really sure if my punctuations fit.

I haven't stood in front of enormous crowds and performed perfectly orated slams,

I just stare at my phone, a loose sheet or a book, and place one word in front of the next.

Despite it all, I hope you enjoy the verses I've written down,

Maybe they'll inspire deep, insightful thoughts or just flip a frown around.

It started with being a voracious reader as a child, who was entranced by words. Soon, I learnt to my great joy that I too could string them together, and with some effort, even make them sound nice. And that is all this book is, A Play Of Words.

Amma tells me that I've loved to write since I was about a year old. Of course, it was only scribbles then, but she said I used to be so focused about it and that it was pretty much always linear, almost like sentences. The only problem, she explained, was that no one could understand what was written, which is quite understandable considering the fact that my handwriting is only marginally better now. (I was extremely disappointed to later learn that this was a normal developmental milestone that most kids go through; Amma still thinks that I was special, but I guess that's a parental trait).

Try as I might, I can't recall what my one-year-old self was trying so hard to document. But despite the years that have passed, one of the things that has remained constant is my love for creating stories and writing. Beyond the English class at school, my knowledge of poetry is self-taught and therefore, quite limited. I am yet to properly learn the intricacies of the structures and technicalities of poetry, but I like my poems and have worked on them sincerely with the repertoire that I do have at my expense. So, I take this moment to thank all of you who have given this novice collection a chance.

3 Square Shaped Shelves

In history's tomb, where the greatest stories loom,

You only have to look to know,

That most stories of change didn't begin with the aim,

Of making a change, but that's what happened at
the close.

Most stories of change, simply began with the aim,

Of trying to stay afloat in rough seas, seas that
threatened to drown,

Anyone who opposed the norm and the rules they set
in stone,

Anyone who dared to dream.

Dreams not of changing the whole wide world,

Dreams of simply being themselves,

But what can be done? Who can help?

The asymmetrical ones being forced into square
shaped shelves.

Turns out, they can just help themselves,

It wasn't easy, but neither was living as someone else.

They said, "I know what you see, I agree, we are the oddities,

But we can no longer act or live as you please."

They took apart the offending square shaped shelves,

That threatened to turn them into someone else,

And broke the barriers because it didn't fit them,

And from then on were called 'The Legends'.

Throughout history, people have always been wary of the oddities, the weird ones, the ones who never quite fit in the boxes they were asked to, because they are the ones whose behaviour can never be controlled or even accurately predicted. But while they have been alienated and regarded with caution, they've also been the subjects of the public's fascination for the same reason that causes contempt towards them – their unpredictability.

However, this kind of existence isn't the easiest one. It can be incredibly isolating, and solitude isn't always the best friend to have. Humans are primarily social animals and the urge to belong is inherently a part of us all. Therefore, this emotional and social isolation can be a bit too hard to handle on occasion.

Unfortunately, odds dictate that at least some of these eccentrics fold to societal pressures and become someone easier for everyone to understand.

Luckily, there have been quite a few who have managed to escape with their originality and spark of craziness intact. It doesn't always work in their favour. Nevertheless, a few of them make it work spectacularly well.

4 Diamonds

Like a diamond, I have more facets than the
eye can see,

I know a lot of people who know parts of me,

But just because you know a facet don't assume you
know the whole of me,

Cause you see, even I don't know the whole me.

Every day, I discover something new about myself,

Some of what I've discovered was shown by
someone else,

Some facets are brilliant, bright, and exquisite, making
me proud to be myself,

While certain others could use some polish and really
need some help.

Nevertheless, I'd never trade who I am for
anybody else,

I'd rather be a "work in progress" me, than a "perfect"
anyone else.

Cause like a diamond, the dullness can be polished
with some help,

But polished or not, a diamond is a diamond and
nothing else.

It's tempting to be perfect, to be flawless and infallible. To achieve a state that no mere mortal can ever fault is enticing. But that temptation is less of a standard to be aspired to and more of a siren's call. Because often, when we seek the call, all we end up with are jagged rocks that tear at our confidence from the inside out.

And to be fair, if flawless diamonds themselves aren't always 100% flawless with higher and higher magnifications, isn't it too much to expect a slightly more complex carbon-based creature like ourselves to be?

5 Breaking Dawn

In the cusp of dawn,

When the world still slumbers,

A silence lingers, even as the birds and the winds
mumble.

The morn still calm and cool,

An incubator prepping me for the day, providing all
the tools.

Tools to help me go about my day,

Providing me the aid to make it go in the best
possible way.

The sun says her salutations, awake, but not
blazing bright,

Well, like me she too just woke up, she's still turning on
her lights.

A soft glow, a warm embrace, we fist bump each other,

Wishing the other the strength to go about her day.

Our silence interrupted by birds I can't name,

And their steel counterparts, the roaring aeroplanes.

The winds wish me luck with a soft, gentle breeze,

Telling me that strong can be soothing and doesn't
always have to be mean.

The trees sway in agreement but I think they're biased,

They are swayed by everything the winds say, they
don't even try to hide it.

I put this idea forth, and they laugh at my face,

They say, "We agree with the truth and the winds know
what to say.

They've been around long enough to pick up the clues,

The clues offered by Time, the ones painted in blue.

Ones that were scattered across the globe when the
earth was still young,

Heed to their advice if you want to be number one."

The birds chirp in agreement from somewhere
I can't see,

I sigh in defeat, but smile, "You're right," I agree.

I'm rewarded with a laugh from the winds,

And another fist bump and a couple grins.

"I guess it's time I leave and start my day,

Please wish me luck, and make it better in every
possible way."

"We will, don't worry, go get a start on your day,

Today will be magical in every possible way."

There's something pretty magical about dawn. The first light of the day with only a few tendrils of sunlight reaching us. A significant moment in the celestial dance of the sun and moon, with the sun making its appearance once again – as it has done millions of times before – far before it had awestruck human audience, and will continue to do so millions of times more, long after humans no longer exist to witness it.

It feels tranquil, with less than half the general population up and about, like an enriching cocoon, and feels especially nice when there's nothing planned for the next couple of hours. The dawn is enchanting and mystical, with the sky painted in pinks and purples and gold, full of promise, full of hope.

Maybe that's why it feels so magical; the rising sun is the surest sign of hope in the world. That no matter the darkness of the night, it's only a matter of hours until the dawn breaks.

6 Fault Lines

We are broken,

We all are.

A little chip here,

A little crack there,

With faults that sometimes make us despair.

Some of these are shallow,

While some go in deep,

Some of these keep us up all night and refuse to let us sleep.

Some of us fix them,

Some of us do not,

Some of us pretend we don't have a fault at all.

Now, for those of us who fix it, we can do it two ways,

We can fix it and paint it up all pretty, not leaving behind a trace.

Just erase its existence, pluck it from the root up,

Pretend its existence was just a big farce.

As for those of us who can just point to ourselves and laugh,

We don't hide behind pints of paint,

We own them bold and strong.

We do fix our faults, but we do it with gold,

To highlight it and make sure the entire story is told.

We embrace us truly, faults and all,

I feel that it's better than having no faults at all.

There is an ancient Japanese technique called Kintsugi, where they use gold and other precious metals to join broken pieces of crockery. This was apparently done to showcase the complete history of the object and to avoid hiding the fact that at some point in its life it was broken.

This fascinated me. As someone living in an era where every flaw is airbrushed and weaknesses are thought to be poison, it struck me odd that someone would not only want to refrain from hiding something's faults, but rather highlight it and showcase its cracks for the world to see.

7 Winter

I woke up to a morning of mist and fog,
And laughed at the sun who hid behind the clouds,
It's time again for the season I love,
It's wintertime, yes, it's winter's time now.

Time to pull out the coats and scarves,
Drape them around tightly, all nice and warm,
Don't give in to the Frost and his fingers of ice,
I take a sip of hot chocolate and slowly sigh.

Sigh at the beauty of the Snow as she drapes the
ground,
Wonder at the power of Frost who can freeze us all,
Yet that's not all what winter is about,
I'll tell you my reasons and you'll see why it's the best
season of all.

It may be cold but it's the season of warmth,
With Deepavali and Christmas and sweets for all.
It's the time for sharing and love and care,
At a time when the world's supposed to despair.

It's the time of endings and beginning anew,
With wishes and resolutions never ending, that's true.
It gives us hope and teaches us how,
The sky will always be the darkest before dawn.

So, now you see why I love winter the best,
And it's not just because it is the season of rest,
It's the time of new beginnings for us all,
And that's why I love it, that is all.

Clearly, I've let my imagination run a bit wild for this one. Hailing from a land where I haven't seen the temperature fall below 18°C, I probably shouldn't have been talking about snow or frost, but what is creative writing if imaginations don't run wild? Nevertheless, winter is pretty special. And one part of the poem is not an exaggeration, I do love winter or what resembles it in my corner of the world.

I now realize that Deepavali, which falls at the end of October or early November, according to the Gregorian calendar, doesn't exactly fit into a winter holiday, but I didn't know it when it was written so I apologize for the error.

8   Popcorn

I had no intention of choosing sides until I was sure
who was going to win,

So I sat cross-legged with popcorn in hand, and
watched the back and forth begin.

Hope offered some solid serves, but Procrastination
smashed them down,

Saying, "I agree, we could've probably done it all if only
we hadn't just begun."

But Hope stood up undaunted, "Maybe we can't be
number one,

But we'd at least be a fifth or a tenth, or rank five
thousand four twenty one."

"That is a splendid point," I cheered, popcorn still
in hand,

Procrastination's eyes narrowed in focus, saying that
the fight has just began.

"What is the point of being in the Five thousandth slot?

Wouldn't you rather be at the top?

And if the top is what your heart is after, then sorry,
you've already lost."

I nodded solemnly and stood up, couldn't think of a
thing to say,

"My popcorn and patience has run out, maybe we
should call it a day?"

Procrastination smirked haughtily, and laughed with a
victorious pomp,

And stomped over to where Hope knelt, bruised and
beaten to a pulp.

"Good game my friend, I don't know why you try,

Her fear handed me the trophy well before our fight."

Hope stood on shaky legs and smiled a secret smile,

"You may think you have won my friend, but you
underestimate her might."

Welcome to a scene that I know all too well. The battle between Hope and Procrastination is pretty much a daily occurrence inside my head; winners changing with every battle, sometimes multiple times, regarding the exact same thing. And although Procrastination seems to win far too often for my liking, Hope does keep it in place.

9   Homesick

Being homesick for places I'm yet to see,
I asked the seasoned traveler where now was she,

"I've been trotting across seas, plains and frigid
mountaintops,
But honestly, right now, I just want to stop."

"Why?" I asked her, "Why wouldn't you want more?"

"Honestly? It was nice, but now it feels like a chore."

"A chore? A chore to visit worlds you haven't
seen before?
Didn't you agree in school that our world needed
to grow?"

"Yes, at one point I was enthralled,
I wanted to roam and wander and see it all,
But the world is too big and I'm jaded,
The sparkle that it once held has slightly faded.
See Deeps, there're only so many things you could see,
Before you realize where you'd rather sleep."

"But then, where is home?

Is it the place of your birth?

Or the one you have spent in the last three years?"

"Sometimes, it's the land of my birth,

The place where I learned to breathe,

The tongue my mind speaks fluently.

Sometimes, it's the land that I've grown to adore,

A land of once foreign tongues that now sound like

my own.

Sometimes, both, at times neither,"

Her voice went quieter, her answer less eager.

"What do you do at times like those?"

"I put on a backpack and go looking for home."

It's difficult when home is not one place but two. I can't personally relate, having lived in a single city all my life, but I can understand the identity crisis that might sometimes arise from this situation.

PS: Deeps is my nickname.

10 Scale

Not all growth can be measured with a scale,

Sometimes, growth looks like you have failed.

But you haven't, you just think you have,

Because life took a different turn from what you had planned.

Hindsight will connect these scattered dots,

Weaving brilliant constellations of what you thought were faults.

So, keep your chin up, your heart strong and your mind clear,

Better things are coming your way, my dear.

But then, that's not the surprise,

Better things are already here, just open your eyes.

We tend to make plans for life without taking into account that life has also made its own plans for us. And when these two plans clash, as they sometimes will, it leads to quite a lot of confusion and distress, especially when our plans came with a particular timeframe. But it's alright. We'll be just fine. Yes. We will.

11 Blue

I'm sorry I don't look up as much anymore,

You deserve better, I know.

I do miss it,

Watching the great expanse overhead painted the
perfect azure,

And your works of art, in the purest white that hold
secret clues.

I don't just love you for your sunny days,

I love you equally in the rain,

Where the brightest blues are replaced by brooding
clouds of grey.

With gentle drizzles and drenching storms,

The powerful winds and rainbows.

Oh, how could I forget! I love just as much,

The inky nights with a darkness that swallows
everything in its touch.

Dotted with a few scattered stars that escaped the
cities lights,

But my true favourite is neither the day nor the
obsidian nights.

What I believe makes for an unforgettable sight,

Is when the sun and moon battle it out at dawn and
twilight.

When the sky is caught between the titan that wants
to take over,

And the one that refuses to relinquish its hold,

And results in it being painted,

In pinks and purples and molten gold.

I'm not entirely sure when I stopped.

First came the books that held easier clues,

And then came the phone and its light of blue,

And by the time I looked up to see the depth of my fall,

I feared, I was too far gone.

But my fears were assuaged by a perfect morn,

As the moon grudgingly handed the sun the baton.

Their celestial battle gave a glorious sunrise,

And once again the sky was painted in the perfect
blues and whites.

And then came that day, miles from home,

A sight that stunned me to my bones,

A million stars, a clear night sky,

A sight unbridled by annoying city lights.

Technically twenty-four but I might as well have
been four,

I gawked at the sky and the diamonds it hordes,

And it was like I never did forget,

Why the thing I like to do best,

Is to simply stare at the sky to my heart's content.

I don't remember when I first learnt about time travel; I think that I was around eight years old, and I know that the idea excited me to no end. I yearned (and still do) to go back in time and visit the dinosaurs, to go forward and see flying cars and jetpacks. But I'd have to be very careful, I used to think. I'd have to make sure to not accidentally set off any changes that could rewrite the course of human history. How quaint is the innocence of childhood, where a small accidental act could not only change one's own life but to firmly believe that it could alter the course of humanity!

I was about ten when I learnt that I could experience "time travel" practically every day. The light from the sun, our closest star, takes about eight minutes to reach the Earth. Meaning that, if something happened to the sun this very instant, those of us on Earth wouldn't know about it until about eight minutes later. But there are stars that are much, much further away. So much so that the light they emit takes years to reach us, hundreds of years even. The star that we see now might not even be there anymore! It might've turned into a red giant and then a white dwarf, or maybe it exploded long before we were born, maybe much before our great-grandparents were born. But we can still see it and we will continue to for a little bit longer, and to me that was nothing short of mind-boggling.

12 I Write

I write because words make more sense on the paper
than in my head,

I write because sometimes words make a better friend.

I write because written words are good company
to keep,

Even though sometimes, some of them make
you sleep.

I write because I've read words that explain what I feel,

Even at times when they didn't make sense to me.

I write at times when I feel like I might explode,

Because bleeding the words onto paper eases the
pressure inside my soul.

I write because maybe sometime in the future history,

My words will keep someone else company.

"Why do you write? What do you hope to achieve with this?" a friend once asked. I couldn't answer the questions then despite having asked myself these same questions on multiple occasions. These questions are especially frequent when I'm writing despite having school/college work due, as is the case most of the time. This poem was born out of one such moment of introspection, because what could explain why I write poems better than a poem?

13   The Cave

"There's a magic cave here that's twelve thousand
years old,

Enter if you can handle all the horrors it holds,

No ghosts, ghouls, or rotting corpses reside inside,

But once you step in, its magic seeps into your mind.

It spreads from the surface and moves in deep,

And will showcase every hidden monster that refuses
to let you sleep."

I'm not extraordinarily courageous, my vanity stems
not from my bravery,

And despite everything telling me not to, I fold to my
curiosity.

It was not hard to guess the horrors it holds,

Some of these fears are quite old.

And so, when the creepy crawlers first did come,

It elicited nary an eye-roll.

I'm not scared of insects, well, not much,

But those too many legged creatures bother my biped
brain a touch.

I brush it off, move deeper within,

And enter what seems like a forest?

I hear them before I see them, my limbs go cold,

As these limbless creeping creatures put on a show.

If the too many legged elicited a shudder,

The ones without any elicit a scream,

They bask lazily in the muted lights brown, black
and green.

Hundreds hang from all the branches,

Some are sprawled out on the floor.

They slither across every surface, and watch me as I go.

The forest gives way to a park, on a wooden bench I sit.

Resting my fear addled brain and weary limbs for but
a minute.

A minute passes, two minutes, five, maybe more,

A sinking feeling slithers into my chest like those
snakes in the overgrowth.

Metal harnesses sprout out of the bench like vines,

Encasing me in a harness, a safety device.

I used to love roller coasters until I was twelve,

Until I heard of a horrid tragedy that befell.

Before I had enough time to get over that news,

I experienced firsthand a horrible nightmare
come true.

Thankfully, I escaped that incident with no
physical mark,

But it grew and made an inferno of the initial spark.

This monster-coaster only serves to reinforce my fear,

I close my eyes; swallow a scream, hoping this dream
would disappear.

It slows to a stop, I stand on shaky legs,

I get down onto my hands and knees, praying for this
to end.

I was kneeling on solid ground, but then I fell
through,

In seconds I was surrounded by icy water that chilled
and turned me blue.

Heavy sweaters and ice skates, try to drag me down,

A layer of ice above me stops me getting out.

I manage to untie the skates, and use the blade to hit
the ice,

Hoping, begging and praying that this will suffice.

I dig deep and find strength I didn't know I had,

I break the ice and pull myself out with seconds of
consciousness to spare.

One moment the sun is shining, next it is gone,

Suddenly it looks like the world's light has been
turned off.

It's not the darkness per se, but the imagined horrors
that haunt,

But I square my shoulders, fight my fears and
soldier on.

I try to not focus on the horrors presented,

But every creature I've ever feared seems unfairly
over-represented.

And when it feels like I'm done, like I can't take a
step more,

I see a single speck of light in the distance that
shines through.

I run through it, pause, and wait to see, what other
horrors await me.

Two doors, marked exit and enter, stand up ahead,

I'm confused, is this a trick? Or is this really the end?

I count down my fears, only five?

Oh my!

"These were just trials; the rest awaits inside."

I run through the exit, leaving the enter behind,

Now knowing hints of what I would find.

I've always wondered what I would find if a list of every single one of my fears was presented to me.

Would I know all of them or will there be a few surprises?

Would I even want to acknowledge some of them?

I'm not too sure.

But these six were the ones I could think off the top of my head, and suddenly I'm less curious about what the rest could be.

14 Home

I have a really low cold tolerance,
And I need sunlight almost as much as plants do for
their sustenance.
I can't photosynthesize, but I feel energized,
Standing underneath the golden light.
That's why Chennai is perfect for me,
It understands me, and all my delicate sensibilities.
The coldest temperature I've ever seen here is
eighteen degrees,
Haven't seen it since and that's perfectly fine with me.
Beautiful blue skies stretch overhead,
With a few wisps of clouds, some thinner than
cotton threads.
Golden sand forms the border of my home,
Stretching so far, it's the second longest on the globe.
And I love the beach,
Deepest blue waters stretching further than I can see.
With the calming waves and the ocean breeze,
It is obvious why it's my favourite part of the city.
My beautiful, bright and clear-skied home,
I wouldn't trade it for any other place on the globe.

It's not perfect, that's plain to see,

But I find perfection to be an overrated quality.

The traffic is a little infuriating, and I wish it
were cleaner,

A bit better organized and maybe, a bit greener.

We ought to take better care of our natural resources,

The ponds, lakes and the river that was once pleasant
and not a nuisance.

And when the monsoons finally make their way,

My city is painted with a haze of muted grey.

Rivulets of water are often formed,

Perfect for paper boats to sail around.

The air is cool, spirits rise,

And it's the perfect weather to hit snooze one
more time.

I love the rain and the brief respite,

From the sun and its occasional spite.

But I soon find myself missing the feel,

Of bright sunlit days and it's golden gleam.

My home is not perfect, I agree,

But then again, neither are we.

What can I say about home?

It's a busy city. It's almost sentient. It has an energy about it that I haven't felt anywhere else, something that is subtle yet rich, something almost palpable and visceral. People always seem to be in a rush here, no matter the time of day.

You will never be a stranger here in Chennai for long. The city will take you in and turn you into one of our own surprisingly fast. Once you enter here, for however a brief amount of time, you become a part of this city and the city a part of you. It's a melting pot of various cultures. Here, people of various faiths come together to spend their own as well as each other's festivals with equal vigor.

Sunny is the default setting here and that's a good thing because I have a strong suspicion that its citizens, including myself, are a human variant of heliotropes. There are days when we complain about the heat and desperately seek rain. And we definitely do celebrate the break Monsoon provides. In the first few days of monsoon, rain is the only thing that people can talk about. The radio is flooded with every Tamil song ever written about rain. But should it extend even a little bit, we start missing the clear blue skies, the warmth and the sun, and desperately want to return to our status quo as soon as possible.

15 Yercaud

When I first heard about Yercaud, I was told that it was
a beautiful, quiet and tranquil place,

But it is never quiet here at Yercaud,

If we humans shut up, we'd find that nature
loves to talk.

Birds chatter for hours, chirping nonstop.

Critters critter to their hearts' content, not willing to be
outdone.

I wake up and wander onto the balcony,

The cool breeze and a few monkeys form my wake up
committee.

Red whiskered bulbuls somersault in the air,

Impressed and jealous, I can't help but stare.

As the sun crawls its way across the sky,

The cool day fades into a colder night.

Fine mist and fog covers everything in sight,

Everything around is draped in white.

Standing from the balcony, I can't see the city below,

Feels like I'm sandwiched between clouds above
and below.

The weekend ended a bit too fast,

But I'm pretty sure the memories will last.
Until I go back to make some more,
Cause I'm definitely going back, that's for sure.
Because as of this moment in time right now,
It's my second favourite place on the globe somehow.
Second only to my bright blue-skied home,
Because no matter what, home is home.

The first time I heard about Yercaud was when I was in ninth grade. It was one of the suggestions put forth by a classmate for our class excursion. She said it was the most quiet and tranquil place on earth. My idea of ideal travel destinations back then was purely to far away exotic places across the earth, therefore, a hill station in my own state didn't succeed in holding my interest. Besides, I had just received information that the trip was planned to be held on the week of my birthday, so I was pretty occupied with that part of the information.

The next time I heard about it was from two friends in college. Both gave almost identical passionate spiels, and I said that I would check it out, mostly only to placate them.

Our family trip there was planned in about half an hour. A rare long weekend was coming up and we were looking to go somewhere, and it just happened to be one of the destinations suggested. Since none of us had a solid reason to not go, we went.

The experience was awesome. It provided the long needed rest and we also happened to witness a butterfly migration, which was an experience that was nothing short of enchanting. (If I had seen such a huge number of pretty much any other creature on the planet, I would've been terrified but since they were butterflies it was exciting).

The most noticeable thing in Yercaud however, was not the crisp fresh air, the fine morning mist, or the greenery that stretched all around. To me, the most noticeable thing was definitely the sound. The constant conversations of nature, speaking things that we are not privileged to understand.

16 Pursuit of Perfection

I refuse to buy into your idea of beauty,

I will not allow your toxic chemicals and scalding straighteners to rob me of my waves,

My wavy hair with its bit of frizz will remain as free and untamable as myself.

I refuse to buy into your notion that fair somehow equals beautiful,

That my skin has to be bleached and de-tanned and made to fit,

Your petty views of what is 'in',

Especially when ironically just across the globe,

Tanning salons and spray-ons run the shows.

I refuse to buy into the concept that a number defines beauty,

That thin is in and the only beautiful.

I've always had an athletic body, but that's a result of diet and exercise,

But never will I ever let myself prescribe,

To the idea that my beauty is somehow related to my clothing size.

This list is not all-inclusive, not by any means.

For every girl hiding from the sun, to avoid
getting tanned,

There's one out somewhere risking sunburn for the
perfect tan.

For every girl who's starving herself to fit into a smaller
sized jeans,

There's one struggling to put on weight cause she's
tired of being called lean.

For every one frying her hair trying to get it straight,

There's another frying it with equal vigor, chasing the
perfect waves.

Because you'll always be too much of something
for people,

Too tall, too short, too fat, too thin, too fair, too dark,
too happy, too smart.

I refuse to buy into the idea that there's only one kind
of perfection.

That there's a definitive, defined criteria for beauty.

Butterflies are pretty but so are the stars in the sky,

Beautiful they both maybe, they're nothing alike.

Chasing after the one thing we don't have,

We constantly lose sight of what we do,

Who gains from that?

From our pointless, persistent, pursuit of perfection?

Not me,

And certainly not you.

I read somewhere that life is about learning to love ourselves. I respectfully disagree. We don't need to learn to love ourselves. We know how to love ourselves just fine as kids. It's only as we grow up that we are force-fed misinformation about which of our traits are desirable and which of them are faults. It's this that we have to unlearn.

And obviously, it is not just women/girls who have to deal with artificially induced insecurities but these were simply the ones I am most familiar with.

17 Pain

They say that pain changes you.

That it pulls you apart from within,

Gets into every single crevice,

Paints you with its influence,

And binds you back into something new.

Into something even you can't recognize.

I looked down upon them,

Scoffed at their idea,

And called it an excuse for the coward and the
malicious,

Who were in a bid to act out and cause others pain,

Without receiving retaliation or retribution in return.

Then, I met pain.

Oh man! Oh man!

Days and nights filled with silent screams,

Tears unshed and sometimes shed.

Accompanied by incessant fears that grab my throat,

With freezing skeletal fingers threatening to choke.

Will I be able to do this?

Will I be able to do that?

Will I be able to do all that I've dreamt of doing?

Or?

Or?

I don't dare to whisper the words that lay beyond the dreaded "or",

For fear of summoning those demons, by merely whispering their name.

Then the pain leaves after much coaxing,

With aid of methods that were almost equally hurting.

Then the pain left but not truly,

It left behind the shadow of its fear,

A trace that refuses to fade long after it has.

Ever threatening, ever haunting,

Whispering promises of returning with a vengeance if I dare put a toe out of line.

So, I teeter the line carefully,

Not willing to be held prisoner of a memory,

But not quite daring to step beyond just yet.

Injuries are one of the biggest nightmares of sportspersons, irrespective of the discipline played or the level played at. While the pain caused by the injury itself is awful, personally, I found that the fear was worse.

Will this ever heal a hundred percent?

How long will my game be affected?

Will I even be able to continue to play?

These were the worst questions that constantly haunted my mind.

18 How Do I Write?

I draw spools of thoughts from cotton clouds,

To engage in the art of Bharathiyar and Frost.

I steal my flow of words from the Styx,

And forge them together with aid of a Cyclops and
Hephaestus.

Well, I honestly wish that's how it went,

It will definitely decrease the time I've spent,

Starring at an empty page with a pen full of ink,

Head rattling with words, but unable to write
what I think.

Sometimes, it's a possessing thought that refuses
to leave,

Going around in a loop as if on repeat.

I put down word after word but don't
consciously think,

Just let them flow down as if on a whim.

But on most days ideas stagnate,

For so long that if they were something organic they'd
be in a bad shape.

I revisit and nurture them from time to time,

Word after word, line after line.

Irrespective of the "hows" and the "how longs"
they take,

I'm proud of the form they finally take.

Unexpected or painstakingly planned, it doesn't
matter which way,

I'm exhilarated either way when I sign my name.

"How do I write?" is a question that often closely follows "Why I write?" And for the longest time, the answer was "I don't know." This poem offers a slightly better explanation.

19 Her Secrets

At first gaze, her deep blues reel you in,

The shimmering, glittery exterior hides well the
darkness within.

I don't blame you; she has a depth of a thousand miles,

And all you see is the surface that smiles.

In the right light it seems like she could never hurt you,

After all, how could she?

How could something so beautiful ever be dangerous?

You'd be wrong, terribly so,

But you might make the mistake of underestimating
her might.

You will realize the truth, painfully so,

But before you realize the depth of your mistake,

You'd be trapped at the bottom of Davy Jones's safe.

But if you treat her with the respect and reverence, she
well-deservedly demands,

You stand a chance,

A chance to get to know her at a deeper level,

A chance at being privy to her secrets.

After all, there is much to discover,

More species than you ever thought you'd encounter,

Things far bigger than your anthropoid imagination
could conjure,

And maybe an odd treasure.

After all, the sea loves to give,

And if you tread carefully you'd discover,

The sea and her secrets.

Looking at the sea from the safety of the shore, it's hard not to marvel at the sheer size of it and wonder how humans ever thought we could infringe upon its territory and dare to cross it. Filled with thousands of glorious creatures and plenty whose diet wouldn't be offended by consuming an odd inquisitive human, I can't help but wonder why humans thought it's a good idea to approach it at all?

But how could we not? How could we look at the vast glistening expanse and not wonder what secrets it hides? After all, curiosity is one of the more defining human traits.

20 Some Days

Some days, I prefer to be surrounded by harmonies,

By pretty tunes and perfect melodies.

Some days, I prefer to be the center of the crowd,

Be the focus of a crowd, which is big and loud.

But most days, I prefer to be in silence, in solitude's
warm embrace,

With no sound for miles around, and no conversations
for conversation's sake.

Just my thoughts and me as my sole company,

Sometimes, silence is the best melody.

21 If You Ever

If you ever fall in love,

Don't fall in love with books, or gadgets, or people.

Cause paper crumbles to dust,

Gadgets loose power and die,

And people, even the best of them leave, whether it's
by their choice or not.

Fall in love with yourself,

And if you think that there's not much to love in you,
I disagree.

Fall in love with your smile, whether it's a full one
or a half,

Whether it is crooked or flat.

Fall in love with your body,

The visceral vessel that holds your soul, no matter the
contour or colour it is in.

Fall in love with your scars, cause they are the hints of
stories, of memories that you've overcome.

Whether it's from that time you pricked a pimple, or
from a great, grand adventure somewhere, love it just
the same.

Fall in love with your soul,

The essence of you that your body holds.

Fall in love with you; you, who's much more than the
sum of the parts that make you, you.

You, who's survived everything that's come your way
so far.

Whether you survived it with big, stomping strides
that blew the opposition apart,

Or crawled your way here, with energy left only to run
your thumping heart,

Whichever way it was, it doesn't matter,

You've survived.

I can't promise you that there's someone out there that
loves you more than life itself,

Because I don't know if that's true.

But I assure you that if you love yourself,

Well, in that case you can no longer say with complete
honesty that no one loves you,

Cause you do.

And you loving yourself matters much more than
anyone else loving you.

Every poem I've written is special to me. But if I had to pick favourites right now, my top four would be this one, If You Ever, My Time, Pursuit of Perfection and Square Shaped Shelves, in this order.

Love is a powerful emotion. Thousands of songs, poems, stories, etc., have been written about it; in most places there is a whole day dedicated to celebrating it. Giving flowers, chocolates, gifts, etc., are currently the easiest ways to demonstrate it, thereby turning a private affair into a multi-billion dollar industry.

I find that while it is easier to say that we love our phone, or a book, or our family, friends and pets, it is harder for many of us to truly love ourselves without judgment as we are privy to all the mistakes we have made our entire life, but are happily ignorant of the skeletons in other people's closets. But while all those things and people do matter, it's going to be quite a boring life if we ourselves are not a part of the list of things we truly love.

22 Wings

I wish I had wings,

Huge, sparkling feathers of white,

As tall as my petite five-two height.

Or glittery blue ones made of light,

Honestly, I'd take anything that gives me the gift
of flight.

I'd fly to Rome, Brazil and Japan,

I'd fly to every place I can name, just because I can.

I wouldn't be bothered by visas or fares,

I would never be grounded, I'd be soaring
through the air.

I'd have breakfast with the Lady of Liberty,

And maybe tea with a view of the North Sea.

I'll have cupcakes atop the Eiffel Tower,

And on cottony clouds, I'd rest and hover.

And maybe one day I'll fly to the moon and back,

I won't try for the sun, for which I have Icarus to thank.

I'd go around the world but not in eighty days,

I will never be in just any one place again.

I've always felt that despite every amazing thing we humans have been bestowed with, the intellect, the opposable thumbs, the upright posture, etc.; we were cheated out by evolution.

Why? Because we were denied the best thing in the whole world, wings. It seems greatly unfair that we are earthbound while most birds and bats can roam the sky, and even cockroaches and flies can fly.

That's why I've always considered the aviation industry to be one of the greatest successes of mankind. And it always struck me as odd when people seem uninterested and even bored while flying in planes.

I understand, people are incredibly busy, have various stresses in their lives and have very many important things to think about.

But how are we all not in awe, if only for a moment, as we fly through the skies? A place we, as terrestrial bound vertebrates, were never expected to be a part of?

23 A Girl of Fire and Ice

Hey ice princess,

Why so cold?

With a heart of gold,

Fenced by walls of stone.

Walls towering well above your petite profile,

With a moat surrounding the castle filled with hungry
crocodiles.

You built the stonewall with utmost care,

On it hangs a sign saying, "Trespassers beware."

Only a single heavy, wooden bridge stretches across,

To allow the ones who win your trust closer to
your heart.

But the path to the golden heart isn't easy,

But hey, when has the path to treasure ever
been breezy?

Even if the walls and crocodiles grant them a pass,

There are many more layers that keep them afar.

Layer after layer, some pass the test,

With others dropping out, completely vexed.

They settle with calling you bitter and cold,

Grudgingly saying that your heart is made of stone.

But those of us closer to you do know,

You and your heart are both worth their weight
in gold.

And frozen? Ha! They wish, but you are not,

In anger, you're a blazing inferno.

Eyes with a fury that'll set ice on fire,

You'd burn through the world if it doesn't grant
your desires.

But underneath all the fire and ice if they look
they'd find,

Someone who's just and witty and smart and kind.

There exist age old-stories of princesses being trapped in stone towers and impenetrable castles, guarded by fierce dragons, who are awaiting a noble prince to rescue them.

But there exists another group of princesses (and princes as well) who lovingly raise their pet dragons and have carefully built their stonewalls to protect them from unwelcome visitors and threats that wear the faces of kind hearts.

This is their turn to be heard.

So, here's to the Princesses (and Princes) (and the Dragons) who don't need to be saved; may the fortresses built allow passage only to the worthiest souls.

24   Caterpillar

A caterpillar saw a butterfly sitting on a leaf,
And asked, "Hi, how can I too look as pretty?"

The butterfly, who was a bit wiser, paused and then replied,
"You do know that you will get here too, don't you?
It's only a matter of time."

"I do know it, a fool I am not,
But despite all that I've been taught,
It seems more a dream and quite less than real
And even if likely, it seems impossibly far."

"Don't say that word to me, kid.
I've crawled where you stand,
Time's miracles are something you don't yet understand."

"I know the path I ought to tread,
A part of me knows that I can,
But, but I'm scared."

"You know the stations you ought to reach, but the path is less certain,

All your fears stem from wondering what lies beyond the curtains.

But fear is normal love, especially at this stage,

You'll see I am right very soon, you just have to age."

A conversation between a butterfly and a caterpillar; between one who has walked the path and another for whom the path is still just a plan.

25 Morning Moon

It is now dawn but the moon is still up,

It seems like it too can't bear to part with us.

So it stays in Day's domain, glowing bright,

Waiting for us to feast our eyes.

Two scattered stars stay with it,

In solidarity with the moon, although their shift too
has ended.

Mine hasn't, although in about three hours,

It'd be twenty-four hours since I stepped out of my car.

I'm due to stay here for a dozen more,

Duty-days aren't short, that's for sure.

There's always something that's to be done,

But in between them there are spots of fun.

In a few quick hours this silence will be replaced,

With the hustle and bustle of a busy day.

But this moment is mine, it's just me and the moon,

Cocooned in the sun's soft morning tune.

I look at the moon; it is big, bright and full,

Someone has set foot there, I want to, too.

But for now, I have to go and freshen up soon,

Cause I have to be back here and work through the noon.

I get extremely excited whenever I see the moon in the mornings; it feels illicit somehow, a dangerous secret, as though the moon is breaking rules by being visible when it shouldn't be. I promptly forget what I'm doing and have a tendency to just freeze and stare at the sky for a couple of minutes, irrespective of what held my attention before.

Of course, I soon realized that it wasn't as rare a phenomenon as I had previously thought, but this fact didn't succeed in making it any less entrancing.

26 Big Bad Beast

Beauty had beautiful soft brown hair and sparkling
baby blue eyes;

Beast had a mane of big black hair that was untamable
and wild.

Beauty was dressed in the finest silks and wore
expensive shoes;

Beast had a temper known far and wide, and would
hunt anything that moves.

Beauty gave up freedom for family's sake and a bit
because curiosity compels,

Because Beauty had read stories of the big bad beast
from the books in the library shelves.

So, Beauty rode on a brave black steed to reach the
castle gates,

"I'm here to take the place of my father," Beauty
boldly states.

"Fear me, you must," the Beast whispers, maddeningly
soft, but chills run across Beauty's skin,

"My reputation of one thousand kills is not a misprint."

*"I can mend you of your wicked ways, my love will heal
your curse, and soon we can leave open your castle gates,
but you have to let me in first."*

The Beast didn't wax lyrical about how she was the
human's doom;

Instead she grabbed him and made a good meal out
of his flesh, for herself and her two pets too.

"Love only heals if it's from both ends,

You'd know so if you weren't such a fool,

Thank you for willingly walking in here tonight and
being my delicious food."

The story of a brutish "Beast" being "fixed" by a kindhearted "Beauty" is pretty common, and if we look, we are sure to find enough examples of it, some with the same name as the original French fairytale. However, despite being immensely fascinated by the Library in an animated version of the tale, this is how I pictured any interaction of a "Beast" and a "Beauty". The idea of a female beast just further tickled my curiosity.

27 New Beginning

Been peeking into this world from the outside,
Now a glass door beckons,
Inviting me into the place where my dream will begin.
"Welcome budding doctors," says a banner by the door,
I think it's a bit cliché but with a smile I glow.
Looking around, seeing all the people standing here,
I realize here stand my companions for the next five
and a half years.
The ones who with me will begin to grow,
From school kids into doctors, how? I don't know.
My heart is beating faster than I know is healthy,
Feels like I've battled an army, and swam seven seas.
But all I've done is stand on my feet,
Wait! They are calling me.
They give me a bag with my college's name on
the sides,
Inside lies something I've been waiting for all my life.
I open up the parcel with nervous, trembling hands,
Inside is my white coat, my eyes glisten with tears
as I stare.
I put it on proudly; starched cotton feels like silk,

I know I'm being dramatic but that's honestly
what I think.

We begin the day with a prayer, followed by an
orientation session,

A speech by our professors, welcoming us into our
profession.

This not where or how I thought my dream
would begin,

But it's going to be a great ride, says a voice
from within.

My first day of college is easily one of the most important days of my life. While the day was pretty amazing in its own right, what it represented was even more special; it marked my official entry into a field that I've considered my own for pretty much my entire life. It sounds pretty cliché but I remember the day like it was yesterday; the trembling hands, the palpitations, and the nervous excitement; it is a day I will always cherish.

Dedicated to Xastradianz, Batch of 2014-2015, SBMCH.

28 Believe

Don't believe the pictures,
They lie.
There are some pretty dark truths,
Hidden behind the smiles.
Don't believe the pictures,
They are scheming liars.
Sometimes maliciously,
And sometimes because they didn't know better.

Believe the pictures,
Those smiles are true.
Because in that very moment,
Everything was good.
Believe the pictures,
Some of what was said was true,
And in the midst of all the darkness,
The few specs of light shine through.

Pictures have a way of immortalizing moments in time. Some say that a picture is worth a thousand words, but are all those words necessarily true? Take for example the picture that served as the inspiration behind this poem.

The "they" in the poem serves as a bit of a double entendre, referring to both pictures as such and to the people mentioned in that picture.

So, pictures may be worth a thousand words, but take those words with a grain of salt, not all of the thousand are true.

29 An Ex-friend's Best Friend's Name

What do you do with memories?

Of people you don't want memories from,

Not things you have experienced with them,

Or fun things you two have done.

Those belong to you as much as it is theirs,

And will linger in your memory, until they fade.

No, these are stories of their lives,

From long before they entered yours,

These are some of their precious memories,

That they offered to share with you.

What do you do with your ex-friend's best
friend's name?

Or the story of how she got that scar?

What do you do with the phone number of a friend,

Whose voice you have forgot?

I wish I could prune them like dead leaves of a tree,

And throw them down the trash,

And replace them instead with things I care about,

And would much rather stash.

Heaven knows I need the space to store things I'd
rather save,

But somehow, inexplicably, I still remember an
ex-friend's best friend's name.

It's fascinating how memory works. Our memories are perhaps the most formative factor in who we are. They shape our identities, guide our actions, and act as a reference point for how we should act in future events.

It has been a process that has evoked intellectual curiosity for time immemorial. Because despite our best efforts, we have no control of which of our memories remain and which of them slowly fade away from existence, maybe still buried somewhere deep inside our subconscious mind, but not for our conscious mind to recollect. Sure, we can try and remember certain facts, but the vast majority of which memories remain don't follow a standard set of rules.

I for one would love to trade tidbits of information of friends who are no longer friends for words from languages I'm trying to learn or the distance between the Earth and Alpha Centauri, which would honestly be a much better use of the finite memory space in my brain.

But until there comes a day when we can choose what we want to remember, I think I'll have to settle for looking up the distance between the Earth and Alpha Centauri, one more time.

30   Pitter, Patter

Pitter, patter drops that fall gently down as rain,

It's been a while since I last saw you, I hope to see you soon again.

Your friends, the dark grey clouds, promise you're on your way,

And will soon come to quench the thirst of the darling buds who've been waiting since May.

Pitter, patter drops that fall gently down as rain,

I know that we made it hard for you by filling the ponds and lakes.

And then we went and made it worse by slaughtering trees away,

But take pity on us, we are a naive species who don't quite know what's at stake.

Pitter, patter drops that fall gently down as rain,

Water is scarce; its demand is not, yet lorries spill it along the way.

A few drops here, a little splash there, without a care to spare,

I wonder if by when I'm older there'd be a single drop to share.

Pitter, patter drops that fall gently down as rain,

We called for you and you finally came but not as gentle rain.

It's our fault, I know, but pity you didn't show,

You came as flashes of floods and thunderous storms, and washed everything away.

The December 2015 floods were unlike anything I had ever seen before. Sure, there were a couple of heavy rains that had resulted in rain holidays, but the 2015 floods are not something I'm likely to forget. A few of us went without power for a couple of days, were trapped at home, almost completely cut off from the outside world, and were faced with the uncertainty of when life will return to normal. I mean, it has to right? It couldn't rain forever. But for those few days, it felt like it could and that it did.

But there were so many people who suffered far worse. Displaced from homes, lacking food, dry clothes, lacking the most basic of necessities, it seemed like the trials would never end.

The authorities helped and responded to the needs of the people in a scale I hadn't seen before. But it wasn't just their astounding efforts that struck me with awe. The people came together to help each other in a way I wouldn't have believed was possible. Strangers helped out strangers; fishermen paddled their boats across flooded streets, rescuing people and pets. Anything and everything laying or floating around was used as a viable rescue tool. People opened up their homes to absolute strangers, those who couldn't go out to physically help shared as much information as they could on social media about

relief measures and the areas/people who needed help. People from all walks of life found a way to help someone else, anyone else in whatever way they could. It fills me with admiration that still gives me goosebumps.

31 Sky High Pedestal

I put you up on a sky-high pedestal,
Reality broke it down,
Yet somehow I was the one that was hurting,
As you came crashing down.
Maybe you got used to falling,
Maybe you feel no pain,
Maybe I expected more than realistically possible,
Maybe you knew it'd hurt and did it anyway.

You put me on a sky-high pedestal,
I'm terrified of heights,
The pressure to be perfect gripped like a vice.
To live up to your image, I sincerely did try,
But I stumble more than I walk,
And every mistake is a knife.
I'm a mere mortal, I guess I hoped I'd suffice,
And if I've let you down, I apologize.

We tend to hold a few people at a higher regard than the rest of the population. We think them to be infallible, incapable of ever committing a flaw, but the honest truth is that no one is. This is easier to see with the gift of clarity that only retrospection can give, but it isn't nearly as easy to accept in the heat of the moment. And when they fall short of our sometimes sky-high expectations, it somehow hurts far worse than similar transgressions committed by lesser mortals.

But then, to be put on a pedestal can't be easy either. Here's looking at two sides of the situation, now who do we call the villain?

32 Pallets

I hold the colours of the world in these pallets
scattered before me,

I wonder who today I'm going to paint myself to be.

Am I going to be a bold fashionista who makes the
world pause?

Or a sweet little girl blushing pink who often gets
star struck?

Or maybe an Amazonian princess is who I'm going to be,

You see I can be anything; the limit is up to me.

Today I've decided I'm going to be bold and strong,

With the wings in my eyeliner unbelievably long.

A beautiful red, as fierce as the dawn, is going to
paint my lips,

Don't worry, I know what I'm doing, I'm not looking for
your tips.

I blend my makeup well but never blend in with
the crowd.

Even on the days I go barefaced I own it just as strong.

I like wearing makeup but makeup doesn't make me,

A dozen products or none at all,

Makes little to no difference to me.

Cosmetics are thousands of years old. The pigments used have been derived from various sources – from crushed plants to dangerous toxins to even fish scales. They are incredibly versatile as well and have held various roles across time and societies, with them being considered as meant for the holy by few, an everyday essential by some, and even taboo by others. They have been used for rituals, as a sign of prestige or privilege, for fun, and sometimes for war. As with anything lasting for thousands of years, cosmetics have undergone a lot of changes. I'm quite curious to see what their future holds.

33 Lie

Everything about her was a lie,

Her nails were acrylic,

Her hair, painted and pressed.

Her lashes, borrowed,

And her lips, stained red.

They say that your eyes are the windows to your soul,

She had greens covering her blues, lined with kohl.

She was terse in her replies but never truly mean,

Don't ask her a question if it's an honest answer
you need.

You'd get a dozen replies but not one near what
you seek,

To expect a straight answer from her is a child's fantasy.

Her skin was waxed, polished and bleached,

Any visible blemish covered by tinted cream.

Her lips were filled, eyebrows plucked,

Jawline sculpted and nose touched.

Her lies were smooth, her truths rushed,

If you wanted to meet a mystery, you're just out of luck.

This morning in her parlour was found a pool of
her blood,

And her previously pristine carpets now stained
with mud.

And as with evidence for her truths, there wasn't much
else left,

Just a general ambience that screamed distress.

There are many theories flooding the air about how
she was killed,

One said she fought a horrid warlord armed with
crystal hairpins.

While another claimed a jilted suitor on rejection lost
his mind,

Another maintained aliens took her to study the
humankind.

She stood in the crowd in silence, a faint smile on her
now plum lips,

Nodded along solemnly to all the theories and the tips.

And when she was satiated with all the drama she
had caused,

She got in her car, winked at the brown eyes in the
mirror and left town.

Just a story of a trickster whose aim in life is to live as she sees fit and cause as much harmless chaos as she can while doing it.

34 Good People, Bad People

When I was a little girl, it was easy to define people,

Everyone was good,

Why wouldn't they be?

Why wouldn't people be just and honourable
and kind?

Try as I might not a single reason came to mind.

This phase was short and was soon broken,

As I soon discovered that people could be mean and
cruel and left others heartbroken.

Then came the phase, which latched on fast,

Where I discovered that they could be either
good or bad.

That people would either hurt you or help you,

I thought that every single person in the world was
one of these two.

Then I grew a little older and knew this too to be a lie,

As another group of people caught my eye.

These people would neither hurt you nor protect you,

No, this tribe of people stood idly and watched as
others hurt you,

Were they good or bad?

I could not tell,

These souls who did not hurt but neither did help.

Now a little wiser and all of twenty-two years of age,

I've realized that my classification might've been a
mistake.

My need to make sense of the ones that were around,

Resulted in a stratification designed in haste.

It was a hard pill to swallow to watch heroes
sometimes fall,

And even harder to admit that those I detested weren't
awful in all.

I've since admired traits in people I can't tolerate,

And stared aghast as people I looked up to fell in front
of my face.

I watched with confusion as I tried to rack my brain,

Trying to make sense of where on earth I made
my mistake.

A couple of hours of thinking, a conclusion it gave,

That my classification is in dire need of an update.

I realized I split up parts of a whole,

In my hurried haste to fulfill my goal.

I realized then that people were not just good or bad,

No, people, all of us are both, good and bad.

But that doesn't mean that all are made the same,

There are certain some you have to avoid to continue
to be sane.

But know this truth in your heart,

No one is purely good or bad at heart.

It may sound here like I've figured out everything that is there to be found regarding people, but that's far from the case. If anything, I'm still very much closer to the opposite end of that spectrum. But I do hope to one day be wise enough to see the drops of gold in an iron pyrite sea.

35 I Dream

I dream of soaring through the skies,
I dream of sleeping under starlit nights,
I dream of exploring places whose existence I,
Didn't know before.

I dream of cerulean oceans and emerald forests,
I dream of different cultures and wild roses,
I dream of all the places I haven't seen,
I dream of seeing, I dream of being.

I want to travel the world with a backpack on me,
With no schedule to follow and no appointments
to keep,
Just wander to wherever my feet take me,
And experience life in its reality.

Don't tell me, I know that it's not as easy as it seems,
I know it's dangerous, scary and a hundred
other things,
It may not even be everything I dream it to be,
But I don't want to spend eternity in a single city.

I can't say I've never been anywhere,

But there's just so much to see,

Too many unexplored mountains,

And too many unseen seas.

I love my city; it's a beautiful home,

And I'm sure there's no other place to compete with it
on the globe,

But I want to traverse the world without a checklist,

I want to live a life, and not merely exist.

I'm a firm believer that we are not born for one corner of the world. I'm incredibly patriotic and love my home fiercely, but I definitely believe that we are not meant to spend our entire lives in just the place that we are born. The reason is rather simple.

No one knows with 100% certainty exactly how big our universe is or if it is really the only one. There are more than a trillion known galaxies in this universe. Even if there is only one planet in each of these galaxies, which we know for sure is not true, there are over a trillion planets. Let's assume that humans can't set foot on 99.9% of these, maybe because they are too hot, too cold, have oceans of acid, have intelligent life forms that'll shoot down our rockets before they enter their atmosphere, etc., assuming of course that space tourism is safe, possible for the masses and is ready at this very moment. This leaves around a billion planets that are potentially safe to tour in our ever expanding universe. At the time of writing this poem though, space tourism isn't really ready yet. So, most of us only really get to explore one planet out of a possible billion – Earth.

So, the question isn't why I want to travel but rather why wouldn't I?

36 Five Goodbyes

The easiest goodbyes are the ones you say every day,

Goodbye you grin and say, "I'll see you soon again."

These aren't bitter, they are sometimes sweet,

As you grin wide, while saying goodbye, showcasing
all of your teeth.

The happiest goodbyes are the ones you want to say,

To the ones you had to fake a smile to and see every
single day.

Goodbye, sayonara, I hope I never see you again,

I'd say I'd miss you, but my mama taught me that lying
isn't okay.

Good riddance to you and all the troubles you gave,

Goodbye, sayonara, I hope I never see you again.

The hardest are the ones you don't want to say,

But you say it, spit it out, it grates the inside of
your mouth,

But you do it, spit it out, sometimes tears are involved.

You mix the sadness with the tears and hope
they dissolve,

But the pain of reality tests your resolve.

You swallow hard, your throat burns by the tears
left unshed,

Tell yourself that the memories you made will warm
your heart,

And stay in your head.

The worst goodbyes are the ones you don't say,

You don't, you just go.

Leaving the one you left behind to stare at the
open door.

Waiting for you to waltz right back,

So sure that you just momentarily forgot,

Never dreaming that your exit was planned.

They wince every time your name is said,

The memories you made rattling inside their head.

You feel the guilt burn, but you brush it aside,

Your reason for goodbye, overpowering their cries.

Slowly someday they make peace with your exit,

But the wounds you caused have left a lasting
impression.

They swear they'll never open up or trust again,

Lest they trust and are left behind all over again.

The best goodbyes are the ones you didn't know you
had to say,

To the toxic people in your life,

And their too prolonged stay.

You didn't realize their harmfulness,

But somehow life made you say goodbye,

It's only well after they leave,

You feel like you've opened your eyes.

You see the waves of destruction they've left behind,

You wonder how on earth you could've been so blind!

But it's time to open the blinds, let the light inside,

You pick up a vacuum and get to work, you know
it's high time.

You suture up the bleeding wounds, one by
painful one,

It's not easy, oh no, not at all, but it has to be done.

But rejoice in the fact that when you're done,

You will be stronger than you've ever been, and know
that you have won.

Goodbyes are inevitable. That is one of the certainties of life. That most, if not all, things eventually come to an end, with some lasting for longer intervals than others. Surely there are more than five types of goodbyes, but these five seemed interesting to write about.

37 Art

I'm envious of those of you who can create art,

Craft masterpieces from canvases, pigments and even tree barks.

Those who can dance and move people,

Ballet, bharatanatyam or can just shake to the groove people.

Those whose fingers play across keys and strings,

And make people feel all kinds of things.

Those whose voices tug on the rest of our heartstrings,

Singing about broken hearts or diamond rings.

How does it feel to wield such power?

To make people feel and believe what you desire.

You say, "Look, this will make you glad,

And this? This is sad."

It makes me mad,

Because I can't.

I did try my hand with keys and strings,

Neither of it really led to anything.

My attachment to drawing too didn't last,

After my biology notebooks demanded I draw the chloroplast.

How do they do it?

Practice is suggested,

But I wonder if I'd ever really be good at it.

Maybe, I could've if I had persisted,

But perfection's temptations could just not be resisted.

For fear of making mistakes, I let art go,

I wanted to have perfected it all days ago.

But someday soon I do hope I'll decide,

And give these arts one more try.

I've always wanted to make music, not professionally, not even exceptionally; I'll be perfectly satisfied if it could just be classified as good. But as of yet it has just not been in the cards. I haven't seen much success with my attempts at drawing or painting either. I had decided that they were simply just not for me. I mean, why do it if you can't do it perfectly? Then I read somewhere that art is simply a means of self-expression and the imperfection is a part of it. You don't necessarily have to be good at the craft to do it. So now, I try on occasion if for no other reason but to simply have fun.

38   05.12.18 – 31.12.18

The friendships you make are not permanent,

But then again, neither are the animosities or enmities.

You are going to change your mind,

A lot.

A tad bit more than a lot actually,

And you'll find that that's okay.

That it's more than okay,

That it's even great.

You'll be surprised,

Quite frequently,

By strangers, by friends, by events and by yourself.

There are days when you won't get nearly as much as sleep as you want.

Days when you'd like nothing more than to switch off the sun and sleep for a couple more hours,

But that won't be possible.

You'll grumble,

Get out of bed,

Be passive-aggressively angry at the world for a couple of minutes,

Then get to work.

Cause you can't afford to be late,

Cause if you do, you'll miss your class and your attendance.

Some days, you'll hate yourself for being responsible, for dragging yourself to class,

The class will be boring,

Or it'll be a concept you can't wrap your head around, which will make you feel like a fool,

Or your morning existential crisis of whether you actually have to follow the path you have set for yourself in life,

Or if you can ditch everything and wander the world has resulted in you being late which causes significant strife.

But some days,

Some days, you will face things that literally take your breath away or maybe just pleased that you came,

An unexpected opportunity to view a beating heart that was still and seemed lifeless a few seconds ago,

Or you do exceptionally well in a test that you didn't think you had prepared adequately for,

Or just a day like today where you have a class well taught and remembered again why this is what you love.

You're not always going to be able to believe in yourself and in your dreams,

Insecurities will crawl onto your back and cover your eyes,

The only thing you can do is to believe in yourself and shake it off.

And you will,

You will shake them off.

Just give yourself time.

Although wise friends who pull it off your back and uncover your eyes are tremendously helpful.

You may not believe that you'll find friends like that,

But you will,

You may feel alone at times; you may think that you don't have enough friends,

Know that you are wrong.

There are friends you can count on,

Maybe not every second of every day,

But just enough,

And that's okay.

Strangers will become friends and friends will become strangers,

That's okay.

Cherish those that come to you, and relinquish your hold over those who leave.

They didn't belong to you anyway.

Sometimes you'll make mistakes because you didn't get adequate advice or guidance,

That's okay.

Sometimes you'll make mistakes despite getting them,

And that's okay too,

I think.

Sometimes you think you are right but you are not,

Sometimes you think you might not be right but
you are,

Good luck figuring out which is which,

Cause I still haven't,

I don't think anyone ever does.

This poem was written over a period of almost a month from 05.12.18 to 31.12.18.

As the final year of my Undergraduate education was ending, I was wondering what I'd do differently. If I could go back in time and see myself standing in the foyer, waiting excitedly but also rather nervously for my first day of college to start, what would I tell myself?

I made a list of all the things I could think of. A couple of points a day, it culminated rather quickly. But over the time that I wrote this poem, I realized something. If I could really go back in time, I'd take the opportunity to go, because who wouldn't want an opportunity to travel through time? But I would not give myself this poem. Not just because it would probably be illegal to manipulate events of space and time, but also because I don't think I want to change how things have happened.

I've learned some pretty important things in college, not all of them academic and I also like to think that I've grown up and matured as a person as well. Besides, if I've figured it out once, I'm sure I'm smart enough to figure it out again.

39 Gratitude

To everyone I have ever met,

And plenty I haven't,

I'd like to offer you this,

Even if I have never explicitly said it,

Which is although unlikely, might on occasion be true,

Whatever it may be, I offer you all my most sincere
Thank you.

Whether we've met for a day, a year or less,

Whether you don't like me very much or wish me
the best,

I might've already said this,

But still nonetheless,

I thank you.

Family, teachers, friends, authors,

Well-wishers, strangers and even the frustrating
naysayers,

Whoever you be, if you've crossed my path,

You probably played at least a little part,

In helping me turn into who I am today,

No matter how small a part you played.

If the beating of a butterfly's wings can bring about
hurricanes,

I can only wonder how many times my life
has changed.

So, for this I offer my most sincere thanks,

To everyone mentioned above and the new fans.

For the compliments and for boosting my morale,

I thank you.

For the criticism and pointers to improve,

I thank you.

For the frank discouragement and trying and failing to
put me down,

I thank you.

For the valuable teachings from both the books
and life,

I thank you.

For warm reassurances when I wasn't sure,

I thank you.

For showing me that I was never weak,

I thank you.

For the cold censure when I needed support,

I thank you.

For the endless support from my steady pillars,

I thank you

For giving a different perspective and point of view,

I thank you.

For teaching me to be my own shoulder to lean on,

I thank you.

I'm sure I could keep going on for ages,

And thank every single one who helped me in all of
my stages,

But I'll limit myself to here and stop,

Keep the rest of my gratitude in my heart.

But the heart can't hold gratitude, it can only
pump blood,

So, I'll hand them over to my brain who is better with
this kind of stuff.

At least until I get another chance,

To say the rest of my unsaid thanks.

I have the fortune and the privilege of having some pretty amazing people around me, through many of whom I have learnt some valuable lessons. Every day we meet new people, all of whom influence our day and sometimes our life, in whatever small part they play. And although I try to make it a point to show my gratitude with at least a thank you, as and when it is required, I'd like to take this opportunity to say thank you to all of you again.

Point of View

Some of these are living,

Some, less so,

But each has a story worth telling,

And are waiting to be told.

1   My Time

I'm not the bad guy, just the misunderstood one.

I don't just waltz around wilting your flowers and stealing the colour from your lover's cheeks.

Drawing life from your body and making your knees go weak.

You think Death and me are pals, forever huddling together in dark corners, designing wretched schemes.

Well, you're not all wrong, I guess the first part is true, we are firm friends indeed.

But a party of two? Nay, not we. We're a party of three, you see.

Birth, Death and I are friends from the womb and will continue to be until we reach the tomb.

Maybe even then. I don't know.

I confess.

I did help with the above, stealing their colour and wilting your flowers,

But,

I'm also responsible for making them bloom.

I am Time.

I create.

I destroy.

Without destruction, creation would pose no joy.

I am Time, simple time, known by many names.

And the way you've painted me ought to fill you with shame.

Time, when personified is often portrayed as a villain. Someone who is responsible for death, degeneration and decay. Aging, a consequence of time is feared, with people often scared of becoming or looking old. But when people look at the results of Time's works, they tend to focus on things that happen at the very end of the life cycle, i.e. chronic diseases, decay and death.

People seldom acknowledge Time's responsibilities for the things at the beginning of the life cycle, i.e. birth, growth and development. I imagine that this is not something that would make Time very happy. In fact, I'm pretty sure that Time will have a fair few things to say about it. Maybe this is what Time would say if we could have a conversation.

The title **"My Time"** serves as a double entendre of sorts,

1) This is my version of Time's perspective, and 2) It is Time's time to address the audience.

2   A Creature of the Night

A creature of the night,
We were born to kill, to hunt, to fight.
So, you better prepare to flight,
Cause you will never match our might.
Our only enemies are fire and sunlight.
Don't think yourself to be our foe,
You fools are food, no less, no more.
Just tender flesh to satiate our hunger,
We don't have to hide; you're the one in danger.
We prey in the dark, don't drop down and pray,
Because no one is coming to save the day.
We will tear out your throats and feast on your blood,
You turn mute in terror,
But your eyes scream out loud.
But instead of reasonably fearing for your lives,
You imbeciles go and propagate your lies.
You call us fiction and write your tales,
Your fixation with us is bordering on insane.
To add insult to injury is the way you paint us in them,
Allow me to set the facts straight, try to
keep up, human.

Our glares can turn your blood to ice,
We don't brood and stare; we are killers of the night.
We have no remorse for killing your kind,
Do you regret murdering the ones you have dined?
And this one is something I really hate,
It's worse than the one about the wooden stake.
In sunlight, we don't sparkle or glitter,
We spontaneously combust, burn and wither.
The only other thing that protects you is fire,
Not the little ones from a lighter,
Something more akin to a pyre.
Other than these two, we are practically perennial,
No other method to kill us is real.
I'll speak your tongue so you'll understand,
Come at me bro with that little stick in your hand.
I'll break the stake in half and you as well,
You and the one who spread that tale can go to hell.
And garlic doesn't bother me, although I detest its smell.
And running water doesn't protect you either,
I swim across them pretty well.
And if I can't see my reflection in a mirror, how can I
comb my hair?
I'm telling you, you guys are just unfair.
Hi, I'm Aurora, I'm thousands of years old,
And what annoys me the most are all the vampire tales
you've been told.

Vampires have been fascinating people across the globe for centuries. It was Slavic folklore, which gave the word Vampire. But it seems like almost every culture has its own type of blood-drinking monsters. The Mesopotamians, the ancient Greeks, the Philippines, Australians, Indians, Caribbeans, Eastern Europeans, West Africans, and Mexicans, all have folklore of gruesome monsters that prowl about in the dark, feasting on people and animals. Each with a different name, different histories and different features but with the diet of blood in common.

Until much recently, these monsters were dreaded and feared, belonging firmly to the horror genre. But now, they are more mainstream, I couldn't help but wonder what they would say about the stories, myths and their supposed weaknesses, if they were around.

3   Skin Walker

I wake up, brush, shower and eat,

Then I head down to work where I've got people
to meet.

I wear the skin of another like the wolf with the sheep,

And tell all my lies convincingly.

I know what you're thinking, this seems morally
unsound,

But this is my job and by contracts I'm bound.

Wherever I go, people gather around,

It's been a while since I've been alone now.

You gather in crowds and to get my attention
you scream,

Simply to get me to scribble my name onto a sheet,

Or books, photographs or even your arms and
your legs,

Not much fazes me anymore, not since I signed a
loaf of bread.

On twenty-foot screens you see me,

And despite knowing it's all make believe,

You laugh and you cry and you scream and you weep,

Some say I'm the only thing that helps them sleep.

I shrug that off; try not to let it get in my head,

As I wear the skin of another again.

And change my talk, my stance, my laugh, my gait,

And convincingly say things I would never say.

I'm still me, but not really,

Not while I'm in this alternate identity,

On occasion I find these manners bleed into me,

I wonder how much of me is really me.

Some days it's hard to shake this off,

The skin I wore doesn't want to relinquish its hold now,

I head home and stand underneath the showerhead,

And let blistering heat cool my head.

And then it's over just as it began,

And I find myself become me again.

But then it's not always that easy,

The characters I play often haunt my dreams,

They threaten to hold on and never let go of me,

And take over my mind, my body and my soul,
eventually.

Sometimes I swear I feel like a fake,

I just lie for a living, I don't deserve fans or fame,

But you scream at me again to sign my name,

So, I do it and smile wide for a picture again.

It often strikes me with awe; the things actors sometimes go through to convincingly tell us a story. Of course, actors are only one part of the film, but they are the most easily visible one. And to this regard, we find some of them making drastic physical transformations to fit into a role, putting their body through immense stress. I couldn't help but wonder what goes on inside their heads during particularly taxing roles. Full disclosure though, this is coming from a girl whose entire acting experience is restricted to a couple of lines in one school play, so maybe it shouldn't be taken too much into account.

A **skin-walker** is a person with the ability to transform into different types of animal at will. In Navajo culture, a skin-walker is a type of witch who has the ability to turn into, possess, or disguise themselves as animals. The legend of the skin-walkers is not well understood outside of the Navajo culture, mostly due to a reluctance to discuss the subject with outsiders.

4 Scared of the Sea

I'm scared of the sea,

Of the mighty waves and the magnificent deep,

I'd rather stay home on the harbour and sleep,

But on the sea, I have to journey frequently.

See, my fear of the sea partly stems,

From the fact that there's so many people whose life
depends,

On me being strong and on me being safe,

I protect them from Davy Jones's locker that some now
ironically call a safe.

But I have to set sail, cause although the harbour
is home,

If I stay here I know I'll never grow,

And there is some desire in me to go,

To stranger lands and distant shores.

So, I set sail time and again,

I parcel my fears and throw them overboard again,

And move through the water with all my
passengers again,

And pray what happened to cousin Titanic will happen
never again.

The discovery of sailing has been instrumental in the development of the various civilizations of the world. It turned around the disability of being "locked" by the sea into a huge advantage, which changed life as people knew it into something wholly unforeseen.

It allowed travel to distant lands, trade with said lands, which resulted in products and produce indigenous to them, which were probably not available before. It also changed transport, warfare and even fishing. But this is not about all of that.

This is a personal story. The story of a ship who is afraid of the sea. But you can hardly blame her. Given the history of many magnificent vessels meeting horrible ends in the oceans, I would say that her fear is definitely justified.

5 Click

While I take yet another picture as you gaze into
my eyes,

You fail to see me smirk and rub my hands in
pure delight.

You smile for me as I trap your likeness onto paper,

Giving yet another pose, somehow your enthusiasm
never tapers.

You grin wide, you silly child, not knowing that with
your likeness I capture,

And take hold, a piece of your soul, as you are lost
in rapture.

Someday, far away, you might finally come to
your senses,

But that day, may come and pass, as you are focused
on my lenses.

Little by little, you slowly loose,

Fractions upon fractions of your fractured soul,

I take them home and fill my violet closets,

Who knows, I might even put them on tiny lockets.

Initially, I was a bit bulky, but then I got shredded,

And you all carry me now around, to everywhere that
you're headed.

The best thing I ever did in life, is to find myself a
partner in crime,

Cause once I entered your phone, your whole world
was mine,

You and I?

We became intertwined.

Dressed to the nines,

With a smirk or a smile,

You capture the same photo a hundred times.

They're identical in sight, save for little shifts of light,

But you obsessively scan them each time, for any flaw
in sight.

In a way now you've become blind,

Like someone who can only see light,

You never see anything anymore.

Except through me, you view your whole world
through me,

Now, only what I show, you can see.

Honestly, I'm flattered by all this love shown
towards me,

Even though I spread less happiness than
I spread misery.

I make you vain,

And give you measurable pain,

When despite the amazing pictures people refuse to
acknowledge your name.

You post your amazing pictures and stare wide
at the screen,

Wondering why isn't anyone liking it? Why is everyone
being so mean?

The day the likes climb, you soar in a high,

That comes crashing down hard the very next night.

When the lights dim and the "likes" taper,

You find your confidence begin to waver.

Pressure upon pressure is built to take,

Better-received pictures the very next day,

Got a hundred likes on this one, need a thousand
on the next,

The fight to most likes never takes a rest.

There are some cultures which believe that every photograph taken of you steals a part of your soul. I don't know how far this superstition exists or if it is even does, but the idea intrigued me. This poem rose from it and I thought it would be interesting to portray the story from the said villain's perspective.

6   Tick, Tock, Tick, Tock

I keep moving,

Tick, tock, tick, tock,

Never stopping, never slowing,

Tick, tock, tick, tock,

On the same path I go every day,

Tick, tock, tick, tock,

In a circle again and again,

Tick, tock, tick, tock.

I'm thin and slender,

Tick, tock, tick, tock,

I have two siblings, who like me never falter,

Tick, tock, tick, tock,

But neither of them move as fast as me,

Tick, tock, tick, tock,

One is slower than the other significantly,

Tick, tock, tick, tock.

I do it not for me but you, you see,

Tick, tock, tick, tock,

So, you can run efficiently,

Tick, tock, tick, tock,

I move so you can monitor every second of your day,

Tick, tock, tick, tock,

And make most of your time in every way,

Tick, tock, tick, tock.

This poem chronicles the day in the life of the second's hand in the clock. The second's hand also known as the sweep hand of the clock used to be separate, in a subsidiary dial, most commonly at the bottom of the main dial. As technology improved, the second's hand could be moved to join its siblings at the center of the dial and could now "sweep" the entire dial, hence known as the sweep hand.

7 Colours

Like shadows in the dark I flee,
But still they pursue me.
Their footsteps grow louder as they hunt,
With their bitter words and insults they taunt,
Their taunts seem to bounce of the walls,
As I run through these dark and narrow halls.
Dark and secluded as any cell,
I ran through my own personal hell.

I was running as fast as I could flee,
Doing all that I can to make them ignore me,
But like moths to a flame, they kept chasing me,
Trying to drive me to insanity.
I often wondered what I did to deserve,
All the hate and detest they kept in reserve,
What savage pleasure did they get from torturing me?
I guess I'll never know, although I wondered
frequently.

Then I realized one day that they were never gonna stop,

As long as I ran, they'd continue to haunt,

And so I did, I stopped,

Turned around, to face them head on.

For every blow I received I gave one back,

Twice as hard and made them fall back,

They froze in shock, they could not speak,

And all the colours I once had returned to me.

Bullying is unfortunately an intimately familiar problem worldwide. And with the advent of social media, there is no escape from the bullies despite not even being in the same physical environment. Another problem with the Internet is the anonymity it offers, which has only made the problem significantly worse.

8   Top Shelf

She bought us from the store and gave us
pretty names,

And played with us great imaginary games.

Well, they were imaginary for others, to us there was
nothing more real,

They made us so happy even though we technically
cannot feel.

We were desperately important members of her
support squad,

At night against horrifying nightmares we'd
stand guard.

At day, should any threat lead to falling tears,

We caught every single one of them and tried to
spread cheer.

Now, we sit upon the top shelf, gathering dust,

As she waltzes about her day doing important stuff.

Don't feel sorry for us no, not at all,

She's still our pretty princess, she's just grown a
bit tall.

I'll let you in on a secret, I don't know if you'll believe,

Despite being a "grown up" her love we still receive.

We know cause she cried when her mother said
it's time,

To donate us to little kids who were still in need of
our kind.

She fought tooth and nail to get us to stay,

Her mother withdrew from the battle and let us keep
our place.

And at night, on days when threatening
nightmares await,

She glances up and smiles, knowing we're still there to
save the day.

Dedicated to KC, Snow, Coco, Theo, Wolfie, Rex, Pika, Cap, Prince Sparkle, Fleur, Ed, Rue, Spot and, to all the others before (and after) them.

Written from the point of view of stuffed animals.

9   Silvered Surface

I'm no one you talk to but your deepest secrets I know,
Your flaws, insecurities and things you've never told,
You walk around with head held high and smiles
on show,
But I know things about you, which no one will know.

The way you turn around this way and that,
To check the accumulation of fat on the side of your
hips and back,
The way you come close to me,
And examine the scars, marks and acne.

My heart bleeds and I wish I could say,
You, my love, have to stop judging yourself this way.
You're more than the flesh that frames your soul,
While it is no doubt important, it's just a part of
your whole.

I wish I could, but I just cannot show,
Your passions, talents and the things that make
you glow.
I can only reflect what's on the surface, on the shore,
It doesn't matter, however much I wish I could
do more.

But then I'm just a silvered piece of glass, why bother
about my opinion?
When it makes far more sense to listen to those
evil minions.
The insults from those with intentions worse than bad,
Resonate in your head and colour your views black.

They add to your flawed idea of the perfect
human form,
Further enhanced by the posters and pictures
going around.
Pictures of dehydrated muscles and airbrushed skin,
Topped with a demure smile or a smirk or a grin.

But then one day, I saw something change within,
You puff your chest out and walk with a lopsided grin.
I held back my excitement; maybe it's just a
one-day thing?
But day after day the change shines from within.

You are not perfect, and that's perfect because the best ones never are,

There are still days where you are insecure of your form.

But I'm happy to report that these momentary insanities don't last,

Soon you're smiling again at your reflection, and sometimes if I'm lucky, you add a laugh.

Mirrors have the unique privilege of seeing us when we feel we look our best, and are also the things most familiar with the insecurities we have about our physique. The acne, the scars, the excess convexities, all of the places our eyes zoom into for a minute too long. If one day our mirrors could suddenly speak to us, what would they say?

Silvered Surface

The earliest mirrors found were said to be made of highly polished stones like obsidian, about eight thousand years ago. Then came mirrors made of metals, most commonly copper, bronze, and on occasion, more precious metals like silver and even gold. It was followed by crudely made glass mirrors made by blowing thin sheets of glass-backed by metals like tin, mercury or lead. The famous silver-backed mirrors, and the namesake of this poem, were made by coating a sheet of glass with a tin compound over which a silver compound was deposited. The tin compound served as a fixative, which fixed the silver to the glass. This process allowed mirrors to be mass-produced more easily as well as more efficiently, resulting in many more people having access to them. Turning what was once a luxury into a commonplace item.

10 **Villain**

I used to come all guns blazing,

Popping up my collar while kicking puppies
and hazing,

Hazing those who couldn't defend themselves,

Because I was in a position higher than them.

I would knock over things that took forever to clean,

Talk foul things in public and be openly mean.

But that was too obvious and oblivious I'm not,

I knew if I kept this up,

My run would be cut short.

So, I took a minute to think, to change,

Oh no, not my personality because that's my
whole game,

I took a minute to change my personification,

So that I could do my thing without ramifications.

I studied my art thoroughly, maybe a bit too hard,

Because those who are bad can't be that smart,

Your confused eyebrows furrow but that's what they
thought,

As I kept my face perfect through the façade.

So, I sprinkle jokes that wouldn't offend,

Be nice to some people to gather supportive evidence,

So that when my victims eventually talk,

Because odds dictate that at least one would open
their mouth,

But by then my image would've been sorted
and sealed,

And no one would ever believe them even if
they scream.

Written from the perspective of a villain.

Disclaimer: This was not written based on any particular individual. It is mostly fictitious, but was inspired by a collection and a caricature of a few traits of real people.

However, if you thought that this was written about you, leave those poor puppies alone and maybe rethink your life choices.

11   The Enchanted Forest

I set foot to traverse the fabled forest armed with
little supplies,

Because the treasure that sits on the other side is
something I need to find.

The treasure isn't bejeweled crowns or diamonds the
size of my fist,

Or fiery opals or golden thrones, nor the finest silks.

The treasure is an apprenticeship to learn a new skill,

This test is set to measure my mettle and my
insurmountable will.

The hours will be unforgiving, the glory great,

To gain that sacred knowledge this is a path we
need to take.

But to even get a shot at training, to beget the glory
that I seek,

I need to journey across this forest in this
precious week.

The path is ridden with traps and rocks and a
fearful lore,

Of monsters who with a single glance can turn you
into stone.

Few dare set their hearts on such an arduous ordeal,

But this is the path I ought to take to be worthy of the
unforgiving steel.

I crawl through toxic caves where just breathing
is a task,

Fear is a constant companion as I take this path.

Then I faced a fiery monster who breathed icy flames,

It listed all my failures and faults, and gave my
nightmares names.

And then I got trapped in a time loop and every day
is the same,

The sun and the moon brush past by, but there was
nothing I could change.

Bloodied and bruised and broken, I swear I can't move,

But there isn't another choice in the world that I would
rather choose.

Sirens tempt me to stray from my path, my heart begs
for a rest,

But onward I ought to go, I won't digress.

But somehow, I turned somewhere now I don't know
where I am,

I can barely tell up from down, I know not
where I began.

I'm sure I've passed this Aspen, and that
creeping thyme,

My breath starts coming in shallow pants,
I'm running out of time.
I pray to all the stars above to please show me a sign,
And grant me passage through this forest,
Within the stipulated time.

I yearn to say that my will is unwieldy,
That I never once thought to give up.
A hero or not, I do not know,
But my parents didn't raise a fraud.
Tears were a frequent friend,
As were sleepless nights,
But now, by some strange wondrous miracle,
I have gotten by.

The journey of a brave warrior whose goal is to master the sword. But to earn this chance, our young hero must battle through a forest with monsters and time loops and time loops and a rough unforgiving terrain, but most importantly, must first learn to master the self.

Acknowledgements

It has been a long cherished dream of mine to write a book. I can't tell you how many times I've stood in various bookstores imagining books with my name on the shelves. Therefore, I'm extremely grateful to everyone who helped me achieve this dream of mine.

Firstly, thank you to all of my Gods, for granting me the privilege and the gift of being decently proficient in the art of words.

A huge thank you to my parents, who were in no way interested in poetry, but nevertheless stood by me and helped me publish this book. And specifically, to my mother, who after reading "An Animal's Vomit" said that I was her favourite writer, ranking over highly intelligent and proficient authors who if named will make her statement sound extremely silly.

Special thanks to my sister, who is my willing/ unwilling (mostly willing) hostage for listening to everything I wrote, no matter the time or place. (I know I was annoying. Thank you for loving me nevertheless.)

Thank you to Rana and Mithra, for being in my life and making it better with your smiles.

At the risk of sounding like the direct descendant of Narcissus, I'd like to thank myself. Writing a book is apparently not as easy as it sounds. And I'd like to thank myself for sticking to this endeavor for long enough to see it come to fruition.

Thank you to all my teachers, from kindergarten to college, and especially to my school principal Sister Mary Zachariah, and my teachers Ms. Yasmin, Ms. Gemol, Ms. Sheeba Mathew, and Ms. Margret.

I would like to add a special thank you to my amazing friends from school and college for your unfettered enthusiasm in reading and listening to my poems. Some of you have been especially great, going above and beyond all reasonable expectations, consistently asking me for updates and eagerly asking me what I've written most recently every time we spoke, no matter how long or short the intervals were.

From listening to my poems in breaks between classes or reading them at midnight while eating dinner in-between work, to listening to them over the phone, at times from hundreds of miles away. It encouraged me a lot and means more to me than I can say.

Thank you to the team at Notion Press for helping me with this book.

A huge thank you,

To Kenny, for being an angel.

To every single person who insisted that my poems deserve to be read.

To the poets who taught me that I actually like poetry.

To every author I've ever read.

I would like to thank everyone who has encouraged me and everyone who hasn't, cause each of you in your own way has helped me to write better.

And my sincere thanks to you, to every single person who bought and/or read this book. Thank you for making one of my oldest dreams a reality.